Hush!

Eka Sunny Akpaidiok

These are my Stories Series
Volume 1

Eka Sunny Akpaidiok

HUSH!
Copyright ©2021 by Eka Sunny Akpaidiok
All rights reserved.
ISBN: 979-8514408870
Published in Nigeria by

Naphtali Books
(a division of Rayany Enterprise)
60, Olatunde Close, Agidingbi, Ikeja, Lagos.
Tel: 2348131978457, 2348136028328

Email: publish@naphtali.com.ng
Website: www.naphtali.com.ng

Hush!

Dedication

To Mummy...

    - She introduced me to words.

To Daddy

He said, "Put those thoughts down, they are called "Random thoughts"".

Part One
Dedication

Hush!

Part Two
Despair

Part Three
Desire

Hush!

Part Four
Dusk

Part Five
Dawn

Hush!

Dedication

Eka Sunny Akpaidiok

Something Beautiful

A Place

Where flowers bloom and grow
Where sea waves toss and turn
Where the sunshine glows till dusk
Where the moonlight ends the dawn

A Time

When palm trees move and sway
When dogs and cats go astray
When people laugh and cry
When others love and die

If we freddie or yuppie
Go cabbage or butterfly
What difference there
If we skated or shuffled?

A Place

Where colours mend and blend
Where lovers mate and date
Where couples match and make
Where friends give and take

Addendum

If we knotted and tied something few years back
Promised our hearts to do our parts
Why go back on our words to spoil something beautiful?

Lagos, July 1990
To my innocent mind then.

Hush!

An Icon of our time: To Our Aunt

You stand tall in our lives
Pointing, prodding, pushing
Believing the best in us
Waiting to see us become

You nurture, tend and care
Treating us each like your own
Not minding what shape or size
Our goofs, failures you see not

Would every family have this?
The better for them if they did
You are our treasure
Our keepsake forever

With what words do we describe you?
Who you are? What you mean?
Our hearts burst, our attempts feeble
We can only but try.

To some you are Big Aunty
Others, simply Aunty Aba
A very strong woman, an inspiration
Loving. Dedicated, a Guiding compass

Our very own Awesome Matriarch
More than platinum you are
Adviser, Confidante, Friend

Showing up for us at all times
A pillar of strength, an encourager
A light to guide, a blessing always
Our Aunt, Our mother, Our Grandma.

Eka Sunny Akpaidiok

For loving us

For believing in us
For always being there
For knowing what to say
Thank you.

As you celebrate:
Let your smile radiate,
Raise the sunshine to see us become
Be filled with strength still for years to come.

Let joy leap from your heart
And put a dance on your feet
You areloved fully, now and always.

Abuja, January 2016.
The Matriarch of the Clan.

FWC @ 20

She grew out of nothing
Tender shoots, budding leaves
Ashes of thoughts on paper
Yet a vision cast on stone

She came borne out of a desire
Souls to save, lives to mold
To give direction, to give focus
To show the way that is right

Like a newborn babe she crawls
Unsteady steps at first
Each day gaining strength
Soon without aid she stands
Heads high, shoulders squared
Always leaning on the One who gives
Boldly she creates, willingly she makes
Dreams come true, destinies formed
Ah! Destinies

Many have passed through her
Like a mother; dedicated
She suckles her young
Tenderly she watches
As they bloom and grow

People, people, people and more people
Forever on her mind
Deeply engraved in her heart
That they may know Him who truly is

So tirelessly, courageously

Eka Sunny Akpaidiok

Stemmed up, trudging on, Plodding

Were there times to give up?
Days without a home,
A shade to shield the sun
A roof to prevent the rain
Death, loss, pain, aches, struggles, issues

Nah!
Great was this commission
This mission, this vision
What it will take,
All that it took
To get the work done.

Two scores and here we are
What a wonder, what doing
Today we stand
On the threshold of something new
Something greater
A new dawn, a beginning again
A tomorrow, unprecedented
Halleluyah!

Abuja, April 2010.
No gates of hell prevailing.

Hush!

Fair Game

Don't take the beauty out of the game
Don't take the shine out of your skill
Compete healthy, fight fairly
Leave us astounded,
Leave us breathless,
At the gifting in you.
We marvel and sigh
Wishing we were you.

Men of old in sporting times
Fought clean and fair
For the beauty of a prize
Heads held high and faces grim
If it killed them, so be it
A name to preserve, honour to bear
They stayed true to the end.

So as you go out to play
Remember from whence you came,
Whose name you bear
Hold honour in high esteem
Stay clean, play fair
Be true to you, have fun
Tell yourself
It's still a game.

Abuja, July 22, 2016
I ran a mile or two in another life.

Eka Sunny Akpaidiok

Karibu Kenya

Kenya
Cold winds and brisk walks
Bodies wrapped up like mummies
Clap, clap, the feet sound
On concrete slabs as they go

Kenya
Cab drivers in white boxes
Awkward left turns and right drives
200 shillings you pay for a drop
"Aah! Me dear, that's a verly good plice".

Kenya
City centre, sprawling buildings
Alas the lost glory of broad street Lagos
Forex huts abound everywhere
72 / to 1 $ you say

Kenya
Chips, chips and more chicken
A lot of bird eating if you ask me
Bland rice and fruity sides
Quick serve they have

Kenya
Pick pockets, they leave you broke
Purse, phone, and passport they take
Rest assured you'll find your bag
Thoughtful thieves so you don't nag

Karibu Kenya is the clarion call
In dark silhouettes they shout out
Pleasant faces and warm smiles
Eager hearts to have you come.

Nairobi, September 2006

Stormy One

I waited for you stormy one
I waited hard; I waited long
Fierce rage
Fiery sting
Biting hard
Against us all

Don't blow off our covers
Don't pull down the poles
Leave the steel boxes
The way you met them

Now you've come
In your usual way
And this May
Ushers you in

Gone are the lighters
Not that they were
Much use at all
A slight whoosh
And puff, darkness looms

The upside is the sleep you give
The downside is the ache you leave.

Abuja, May 2016

Eka Sunny Akpaidiok

Hooked

Came across you through a friend
Chats, texts and calls paved the way
Then I saw you and fell
Stretched my hand and held

Love is seeing
My eyes wide open
Like firefly to light
I drew to you

If I were asked
I'll say a few and more
Caring, selfless, focused
Convinced I am about this

Hangouts, indoor curled up
Let's gaze into each other's eyes
Grin and be lazy
The world, ours, our love pure

Your lips on mine
Gone is my breath
Let me drink of your love
Be lost in your embrace

You are mine and I am yours
Hold me don't let me go
An exciting journey
We have ahead.

Abuja, December 2016

Getting Married

Refrain:

For better, or worse
For riches, or poorer
In sickness and in health
Till death do wepart?

Far way west
Went something best
A bride with pride
Was married in stride
Giving away a bride
With so much pride
And such was the price
Which was paid in thrice

The organ was struck
Then went the truck
She with her father
Without her mother.

Lagos, July 1990

Eka Sunny Akpaidiok

Honour

Our heroes while alive; honour
Their songs loudly; sing
Soon it will all be over
We are left with regrets

Their deeds clearly; tell
Praise where due; give
Applaud and shout
Share a story or two

Reminisces are for later
When all is said and done
Six feet down we go
Let's not wait I pray till then

Our heroes while they are here; honour
Unsung stories are made for print
A pat on the back
A high five slap
A thank you
A well done
Nothing too great
Nothing too small

Our heroes now not later; honour
Regrets are for fools, excuses are that

Tell your father's deeds now
Sing your mother's praise
Love your brother, hug your sister
Share a date with a friend or two
Don't wait for later
Don't wait till then
Do it now, Do it here
Soon their gone,
Like the wind…

Abuja 2014.

Hush!

Happy Birthday!

Birthdays are for moments, joyous and free
To be grateful for all we are allowed to see
To reminisce and testify, for wishes,to dream
To laugh, share, dance and eat white cream.

Stop and put aside your busy schedule
Take a deep breath, blow out in full
Think of all they have been to you
Let them know in words and deeds too.

The Miracle of birth, a newborn inside you
Wait, Look, and see a mini you.

Abuja, January 2017

Eka Sunny Akpaidiok

My People

I know a people of a certain curious breed
Tenacious, strong, bold; of such holy creed
I know a people who laugh at danger's scare
They dare push forward because they do care.

I know a people who will pull down a stronghold
With arsenals that are really amazing to behold
I know a people, faithful, committed and funny
They leave you in stitches laughing on your fanny.

Challenge these people not
Don't even dare I pray
For soon enough they rise
No matter how gray.

You define the word unity
You make together sound sexy
Tenacious looks simple
And bold, still a strong word

You are the true reflection of love
And "we care" no longer a cliché
Relentless is the latest in town
You are these and much more.

I know a people...FWC Worship Team...my people.

Abuja, March 2019
In a smile and a clutched heart
I remember.

In a Heartbeat

How do you stay for two decades?
How do you put with all the shenanigans?
How do you smile and nod away at some nuances?
How do you not grind your teeth and not pull out your hair?

If not that:
Grace smiled down at you
Love filled your heart
Gave you wings to fly
Faith said 'keep at it
Finding each other was all worth it'
Hope stirred the dreams you dared to have
The journey stretched out; far before you.

You found your perfect fit
You'd do it again in a heartbeat

To Him who has allowed this to be
To Him is all the glory.

Abuja 2018

Eka Sunny Akpaidiok

Love Notes

I see the sunshine on your face
I see the wind draw out a trace
Of beauty personified
And Grace classified

Your kind is rare, your mix has flair
Your gait I admire, your stance is clear

You are bold
Even when told
You are fun
When no sun

Beautiful. Humble. Bold, yet gentle
Firm. Kind. A Calm Listener
Generous. Not Showy, A wise teacher
Nobody need know what you do for others.

Abuja 2018
My heart is allowed to dream
Yes, my heart.

Hush!

Supporters Club...

Our young men came
Cajoling and pleading
Got us all committed
We came out in droves
Just a lil' above twenty
We drowned the *vuvuzela*
With our one thousand voices.

There were no second takes
No rehearsed speeches or lyrics
There were no second service make-ups
Nor time for major or minor keys

It was fun, it was silly
There was laughter and local lingo
We brought the house down
With our crude *Stellar* performance!

The game had dribbles
Some brilliant giant saves
Many awkward falls
And local parlance "*waste pipe*" moves!

The camera holding men
Amused and bemused
Were left quite amazed
At our unrehearsed antics.

The first goal came
Got us all sobered up
I tell you the humble pie
Never ever lies.

They hooted with glee
They mocked at our quiet

Eka Sunny Akpaidiok

Made feeble attempts at sound
But you can't keep us down
"Why look for the living among the dead?"
We rolled out the drums
And raised our tambourines
Like David, Joshua and fine looking Miriam
We slayed the giants!

Unknown tongues made it to the arena
Christie's chips made it too
Uncle Master's wife gave drinks
An unplanned party!
What more could you ask?

Every soccer chant ever known
In lead vocals and amateur DJs
Progress and *Dora* leading the way
There and now*Soso* would raise
In that sexy silky voice
Not suited for such crowd
Onome; a tune and a dance
Jojo in some local ballads
"Cassava legs" and the like
We dared mocked with this once
Uncle Master took the chair from the *WD.*

I could go on, but I'm plum beat
My voice hoarse and eye lids heavy
Never have I let go in so long a time

One apiece it ended
God of soccer ever so just
Every side a winner
For their sakes I'm glad.

Next time when they call...you might want to come out
Cause I can't quite capture all on pen and paper...scratch that...on android!

Abuja, April 2019.

Hush!

Woman

Preconceived ideas blur the lines of reality
How well she lived you can't perceive
Till she lets a window of her life open
Scales of ignorance drop when you listen
To her unsuspecting start of life
Follow the path created, drink from her knowledge
She juggles varied roles without missing a step
She stands out like a beacon of hope, unassuming
Virtuously laced with class, style and great grace
Exuding an aroma of praise, truth and delight.

Much more than the nectar down there
Much more than the thighs and hips
Much more than the melons that sways
Much more than the tips and lips

Though they beckon and invite
Though they speak too loudly

Be comfortable in your own skin
Don't look to the other in despair
Your frame is not shaped like hers
Some come tall, dark and skinny
Others round, smooth and shinny
Carry yourself, hold your head high
Remember there are not two of you
No mistake made with you created.

Abuja, November 2017

Eka Sunny Akpaidiok

Away!

Away, away
Go your different way
If your heart be weary
Worry not a nary
At the Father's feet
We all still sit.

Away now I say
Our path a clear way
Yield to the beat you hear
Fret not for all is now clear.

May love be seen in this new
Whilst we seek to fit and blend
May our spirits refresh anew
As our hearts beat and mend.

Abuja, May 2019.

Hush!

Drama!

Somebody told
Somebody sold
Somebody bought

They guarded my house
And thought me asleep
I laughed as I stole away
Deep into the night

They can't be that inept
These men in black
Who guide as they teach
In rough sounding speech?

Somebody told
Somebody bold
Somebody smart

We watch the drama unfold
And I ask those of long old
Is there anything new?
What the heck is all the hue?

'Cause I've come to show
I'm better at this game than you
If you let me teach a thing or two
You will learn and pick up the flow.

Abuja, July 2018

Eka Sunny Akpaidiok

One Black Nation

The law is your friend
Not so much here following the trend
A few good souls though they are
Who utterly refuse to go with the flow
The other day they got us wondering
When the Chief started stuttering
A written speech that had him confused
Over a subject on being transfused
We are special breed
This black nation we call ourselves
You'd think we live by no creed
Never afraid to come off the shelves
Fickle a lot of the time
Belittling all in every possible clime
Whisking away all daunting matter
Finding ways to create more laughter
Unwritten we are the happiest
All is a joke no matter how feeble
Blame it on the ***Oga*** at the top
Who knew not where his web ad went!

Abuja, April 2019

Hush!

Survive!

A carrier of pain carved out
Hope is lost so the story goes
This curse, mine to inherit
I see no way out
Why look at me with empathy?
Can you carry the cross I bear?
You think to sympathize with me;
You attempt to show you care
I am bent out of shape
This pain takes the credit
Fight the fight with all of my might
Echo the litany.
My utter weakness hidden
In my bold bitten lip
One word slips past,
Clenched teeth and fist
Raspy breath, doubled over
One word…

Abuja, March 2019

Eka Sunny Akpaidiok

Aah! Smallie!

Sassy Spunky.
Bright Bold.
Cheerful Charming.
Funny Faithful.

She smiled with her eyes
She laughed from her heart

Like a breeze
Like a breath of fresh air
No dulling with her

There yesterday, gone today
Taken out of our hands
No time for good byes.

Abuja, December 2018

Despair

Eka Sunny Akpaidiok

Hush!

There is:
A journey through a dark place
A brooding over a dark time
A hovering over a dark space
But silence keeps the light out.

There will be:
Moments of many lows
Times of hunger passing slow
A yearn for the other lacking
But silence keeps the light out.

There is:
The lonely trudged road
Burden bearing that only goad
A searching; pridelet's not up
But silence keeps the light out.

Hush!Shush! Don't speak up
For each one bears its own cup
Hush! Shush!Don't let it out
But silence keeps the light out.

Life:
Journeys through a dark place
Broods over a dark time
Hovers over a dark space
And silence keeps the light out!

Abuja, May 2019

Hush!

Where do I belong?

I walked into my domain
I looked into all the rooms
I knew every inch by heart
I had dreamt its birth from start

I stood on the patio
Asked myself
"Do I belong here?"
"Is this my place?"

I stretched my mind
To remember the past
For here my dreams
Had taken on wings

Wafts of smell beckon, drawing me,
Drugged, I followedscents so heady
I entered a space, a satisfied smile
Manymouths served from here

I hear a sound tumbling, falling
Thud!Thud! Patter! Patter! feet
I dash out to catch perhaps a fall
It's another space, I sigh, little feet

Time has flown without a thought
How I waited for these to come
Some laughed, mocked and questioned
Why couldn't I like everyone else?

Today the story is different, the wait gone
I bend to pick the litter here and there
Tiny feet wrangle round my sturdy ones
I muse on the Faithful One who bided His Time

Soon there is quiet and I drag my feet
To the safe place I feel always

Eka Sunny Akpaidiok

Open space, no clutter; peace
Hide what should not be seen

Still I sense a foreboding
"A stranger in my domain?"
Every room should be mine,
Every space I have occupied

They try hard it seems from what I see
To confine me to a space they think
To a mold they have created me to be
Freedom floats in my mind, see

Perhaps I don't truly belong here
Or better still I belong everywhere
Answers sought to the musings
Silence! Made to feel small.

Abuja 2016

Rampage

Again it started just like that
Before a word uttered
Boom!

They called it mid semester break
And planted rocks that looked like men
With guns and batons and another called teargas

They sent us out more like sheep without shepherd
Cows, goats going astray, they sent us out
"Hey! You there, over there, double up
Come on you there, hands up, roll."

Bag and baggage, cars and carriage
Packing, hoofing, looting, stealing
Hurry, quick, adrenalin flowing
"They're here", "I'm going, I'm coming"
Gone!

Calabar, June 1993

Eka Sunny Akpaidiok

Trumping

He could
    He just could
Scary thought
  Shivers just thinking
Don't go there
But what if
     Horrors!

Nightmarish pain
Darkness groping
Denial
     No
     No
     No

But what if
    What if
What if
Echo
Whisper
  Nooooooooo!
    No!

Breakout
Cold sweat
Goosebumps
Something walked
 Crawled rather
Over my grave

What if
He could
He just might

Puling covers
 Darkness

Nightmare

Hush!

Noooooo
Wake up

He just might
Echo…

He did!
He trumped!

Abuja, November 2016.
The time moved in our minds
Much too slow for many.

Eka Sunny Akpaidiok

Stay?

I put up with your mindless games
Indiscretions that leave me breathless
Your disdain one too many
Fooled from the start I saw me in you

Many have told me to up and go
To leave this life that looks like a past
To shun the shame and somewhat disgrace
My dignity trampled is not worth it

I put up with the insults and mockeries
My self-respect no longer worth a penny
I am shunned outside like one without fiber
I have left this too late, the taunts reecho

I turn and try to see past the thick fog
I hold onto a dream fast fading away
In the glass are fragments of my heart
In fragile pieces, scattered here and there
Yet stay I do in this unclear path
Time is gone the minute I awake
The brightening of the star fades away
I caught a glimpse of what should be
The greatness that so seems to elude
But stay I would, my cross to bear.

Abuja, 2016
Merchant ships escape my grasp
A path not clear eludes.

The Agenda?

We hear a sound from far away
Drum rolls and clanging cymbals
Whistles blowing, detached notes
Thumps on the ground, heavy beats

We hear wailing and crying laced in despair
Anguished descants, shrilled at the end
Gut wrenching, sobs, shuddering shoulders
Babies ripped out of protruding bellies

Fires gutting down what took years
Ferocious flames leaking up water
Accusing eyes, as papa runs away
Families left, abandoned, alone

Betrayal, denial, lies, mistrust
A world collapsed before our eyes
Mouth agape, no time to exclaim
We must run too or be caught in it

Five men fell on top of her
Ripped off her garment and took turns
They laughed as they thrust
Blood sucking demons
Unleashed without restraint

Brother turned against sister,
Husband denied wife
No friends, neitherthe friendly enemy
Cocked guns, grenades, sharp shooters
Clubs, knives, javelins and hand slings

We looked past what used to be
Tall, beautiful and intimidating
Now burnt to ashes, its embers still aglow
Slowly it crumbles becoming dust

My feet are not clad: stones prick, hurting me
I am exhausted from running, trying to get away

Eka Sunny Akpaidiok

I thirst deeply, and indulge in a minute of fantasy
I remember my refrigerator with longing.

Night-nappers

Night brought this deafening noise
Clubs, knives fierce looking jagged edges

They were rough
They were callous
Our pleas, Our wails
Fell on deaf ears

They took the young
They spared not the old
They dragged the reluctant
And wasted no time on the weak

They pushed and shoved
They kicked and head butted
They were wild, they were cold
They hungered for blood
Like vampires of old

They maimed as they struck
And took captives with them
They separated, they tore apart
They put the sword and divided us

We ran as we could
We fled for our lives
"Stay alive,"
"Don't give up"

Did I stop to think?
When would I see home again
A faraway thought
Wishful thinking.

Abuja 2016.

Eka Sunny Akpaidiok

Lost World

The world is sick
Thinking it without a cure
But the Healer stands
Within arm's length
Waiting...

The human heart
Boils with rage
With deep hate
For revenge
Over a fight
That is not hers

You don't like my face
You hate the stance I take
Does not give you the right
To snuff out my life

Soon they will gather like vultures
To poke around
To ask why, to ask why
To seek for answers
That stare us right in the face

I am black, and you are white
You tan, I darken
I am red, you are yellow
My hair is black and straight
Yours is wooly and bushy

What evil rules the heart?

Hush!

What rage snaps the mind?
What poisonous venom in the blood?
What rancid breath I perceive?
What despicable act?

Dangerous weapons
Weapons of war, assault weapons
Hand guns, grenades, rifles
Shooters, terrorists, murderers.

Cruel words and hate speech...

Abuja 2016.

Eka Sunny Akpaidiok

A Changing World

In a world where long gone
In the right and in the wrong
In a place where truth is uncovered
Lies don't hide behind the corners

In a world soon fading away
Where a man marries a woman
From the beginning it was so.

The weather changes
The people do same
The young calf now;
More valued than you.

In a world where I find me
Where right ceases to be
And wrong is winked at
Nothing is hidden anymore.

Abuja, 2016.

Heat
Sweaty faces
Sticky bodies
Stifling, irritating
Annoying, unbearable

No mercy, No pity
Hot rays shines on

Snappy moods
Parched throats
Short tempers
Itchy bodies
Smelly odors
Cold baths
Restless nights
Spinning blades
Hot air.

February '98

Eka Sunny Akpaidiok

Crikity, Crakity

To the south I intended to go
Thus by road I journeyed so
By bus we packed all tight
Harrumph! It didn't look right
Alas! We had no weary say
By road the only one way.

Prayers said and good byes made
We started out as we were bade
I steeled my mind, and twisted on my seat
No strength I find, it was no small feat.

Kai! Our roads are bad!

But here I go,
Well ahead of myself
I am here to tell a tale
Please bear with me
As I take you on a journey
By dreary ole' road you see.

Many a times we plum forget
How beautiful this nation can get
Thick dense forests, huge hewn rocks
Brimming with life, verdant oh so green
Tall trees with the perfect barber's cut
Fords, streams, rivers, waters cascading

The ride was bumpy, the driver hmm!
Dexterity was the name of the game
He swerved and swooshed
In the bid to miss the pots
So we bumped against oneanother
As whiffs of smell assailed our nostrils

Road blocks, check points and the khaki men,

Hush!

Part of this tale they are I'm afraid you see
Crude looking riffles, and rough sounding speech
They made an interesting study as we sped away

Dark as midnight were some of them
The sun had done its fair share of tan,
Others with yellowed teeth, and cracked lips
Not a pretty sight to behold, these khaki men!

"Your particulars" (grimace) now a popular song
For formality sake, so to speak
Cos the driver knows what to do
"We are in haste, our journey far"
An outstretched arm; a palm is greased

"Why do they bother?" I ask myself
No search is done, no paper seen
A nuisance they've become
A menace too, what use are they?

Urchins rush by as we are stopped
A sale or two will make a difference
Food on the table, money in the pocket
It's a week day I note, they are not in school

Soon we stopped for lunch or brunch I think
Ten minutes, the driver states not a minute late
Out we go to find what to eat
Other travellers too, a beehive of activity

We are back at it again, and just when you think
You've made some miles and eaten up space
Crikity, crakity, a noisy sound, swoosh, swoosh
Air let loose, to a halt we've come, to go no further

Groans, wails, a pouty face, a child yelled out
This was not the plan, you see, certainly not

Grudgingly, stubbornly, tiredly we filled out

Eka Sunny Akpaidiok

What fate awaited us in this journey so far?

I looked up at faces grim, sore and bare
Could trace a trickle of dirt here and there
I almost guffawed with mirth looking at them
Humour will keep me sane just like a balm

The driver humbled not a word he uttered
Stepped out for help in this far remote place
I looked around and wondered where we were
Nothing much but trees and few mud houses

So we got talking and introductions were made
We encouraged ourselves, "the driver will come"
With help for all andget us back on the road
An hour or two had gone by, no driver in sight

Soon enough the shadows of dark fell
Casting worried looks, frowns and hisses
Gloom had settled even the cheeriest despaired
Still no driver in sight; 5 hours gone now

I was hopeful and made my confessions bold
All I learnt in church was coming to bear
But "Faithless" (I called him) just would not let up
Spoke of doom, and despair, of darkness and fear

'Hush', I almost hissed. 'Back to sender'
A damper on our spirits 'Faithless' had put on
Dark shadows loomed with no hope in sight
Our tummies rumbled and growled two meals late

The bus searched and a tuber of yam found
A fire we got blazing; roasted yam for dinner
We fell on it like pack of wolves, niceties aside
Nothing tasted so sweet; hunger makes even grass…

On Nigerian roads, 2015
To be continued…

Hush!

Subsidy Part 1

Someone explain this subsidy thing to me
'Cos I'm tempted to think it's a Nigerian word
Someone explain this subsidy to me
In plain simple English terms

Someone explain this subsidy thing to me
For there are five widows in my father's compound
Someone explain this thing to me
In a way they too can understand

How do you explain a journey once *N150* yesterday
Now *N400* at the same distance today
Last we checked, nothing had changed
Not the road, not the means, but the subsidy!

Someone explain this thing to me!

Abuja 2015

Eka Sunny Akpaidiok

No gain in Pain

The tide has turned again
This time with much pain
The beats roll, I see no gain
In this bloodletting grey rain

How do we sing our song?
And dance all night long
To the beat of the gong
With its hollow dong

Our land our sand
We wail, we hail

My loss, our loss
Your pain

Let our land receive your mercy LORD.

Abuja, June 2018.

Different?

Why seek to compare
With reasons not fair?
Cultures differ
Here and there
Moot points and analysis
Bereft of true basis

Look to you, and be true
Right your wrongs still blue
Retreat from the path of same old same
They are who still play the blame game.

Abuja 2018

Eka Sunny Akpaidiok

Absentee Masters

Learn a thing or two the wards tout ever
But the masters concerned are never there
Forever they lay tools down and seek wants
We spend years on end without learning
Any wonder we come out not so bright
Truth be told, not a letter can we pen

The other day we had it up to here
So off we went and called on the gods
"We would have a sit in, we would pray"
We got a seer, a prophet and a priest
We created fliers and handed out
We irked from the mess, tired too
We tagged our cause "*ASSU wetin we do you?*"

Abuja, 2014

Hush!

Dare

Dare I ask why?
Would I be that bold?
Answers I seek
To the thirsting of my soul
I toss and turn, hiss and sigh
I shudder at thoughts
Torment my mind

Dare I ask why?
And darken counsel
Without reason
He who made the storms
That rage within
Allows a life
Snapped up too soon

Dare I ask why?
Screeching at the
Top of my voice
A huge need to vent
To wail out my pain
Didn't we do enough?
What more, I ask?

Drenched in tears
Heavy hearts
Anguished faces
We smile through
Pain and all,
A silent scream
Cos we know
Him who knows

I know not enough
I can never out do Him

Eka Sunny Akpaidiok

He knows
This All Knowing
He sees, far and near
From finish to start
He exists always
Infinitely

Rest for the one gone
Too soon, they say
A race finished
A course ended
Rest, ache no more
Dear one
Rest.

Abuja 2015
Despair

Hush!

The Me YouSee

Do you need another to affirm?
Do you not see in the waters?
Etched in your reflection
A beauty that will not fade

No, you see what you hear;
"You cannot", "not good enough"
It echoes loud and clear
You are deafened by the sound

But, today I hear differently
You call me beautiful and alluring
You say I'm soft spoken and gentle
I am tempted to scoff; "if only you knew"

You say I am strong, bold and loving
I can do anything if only I try
You push and prod; you are patient with me
You see what I don't see.

Abuja 2017

Eka Sunny Akpaidiok

For Ugbo
The morning light is gone
The evening tide is yon
Snatched away too soon
No time to sing a tune

Would not dare ask
This rude awakening
Will not wonder why
A quiet nod is all

This surreal feeling
This uncertainty is
A life lived well
Will no more tell

Tell your tale while you can
Sing your song, play your can.

Soon…

Abuja, January 2019

Hush!

The Sound of It

It comes everyday
A moment
A flicker in time
Unrecognizable…always

Shrouded in a cloak
Of dark evil hue
Covered in empty pans
And bare pockets

Layered in white sheets
And ailing bodies
Scattered in twisted turns
And upturn vehicles

Full in hungered faces
And growling tummies
Clustered in green eyed
Monsters of envy

Lurking in closed mouths
And a troubled mind
Baring uneven teeth
And stretched clawed arms

The sound…

They whispered "No
You will not have me"

Be wise to see the Shades of colour
Recognize its Shapes and sizes!

Abuja, May 2019

Eka Sunny Akpaidiok

This Mortal Body So

This mortal body so
Will one day up and go
Without as much as a good bye
From where it yet may even lie

Find it hard as it may be
The time comes for all to see
Tidied affairs; a house put in order
Makes haste as it goes to the other

Hold lightly the things you have now
Naught will leave with you anyhow
Neither the fame nor the pride
Even if acquired with great stride

Vultures gather for plunder and spoil
Not one day spent in sheer hard toil
Lines of greed unmask ones true intent
I see their crazed looks all hell bent.

Abuja, February 2019.

Desire

Eka Sunny Akpaidiok

Flutter, Flutter

Today
You loved me
You loved me well
A smile on my face
Huge as the sea
My heart flutters
Just thinking of you
All these made possible
By the Father's great love

The night is fast gone
Soon it will be day
I shut my eyes
Thinking of today
All I can say
You love me
You loved me well.

Abuja 2016
To my friends and the tale
Of seven pillows.

Hush!

Please

My heart beats for war torn countries
For glories brought down by the greed of men
Of little ones, and horrors they have seen
Innocence lost, Trust betrayed, Hope defeated

Faith frayed at the end of the seam
"Why do we fight?"
"Why do we war?"
"Can we not lay arms down and talk?"

Our world is gone because we listen not
Our beauty fades as our skin shrivel
Some dreams shattered even before birth
Pain, chaos, turmoil and utter despair

Pick up the pieces, the future now
A new leaf sprouts, fresh and green
Don't let this darkness eat you up
Refuse, reject, resist, renounce.

I long for a time of easier moments
Of days with peace and moonlights
Our feet drew castles in the sand
Washed away by rushing liquid fire.

I long for days of unending laughter
Of noisy playlets and cheeky games
But you would not stead you war
Selfish gains and lofty missions.

Abuja 2016.

Eka Sunny Akpaidiok

You and Her

And the Lord made you and her
That you walk by her side

And after being friends
He made you and her

That when together
You are one.

Calabar, April 1993

Waiting

She sat on the lattice
Smelled the daisies
Stretched out

Look, my love comes
Towards me
I hold out my hands
In anticipation?

Panic rises within me
It rushes at the tip
Will my love come
Would I still wait?

Be still my beating flesh
Rein in the rush
Reveal no hand
Let not the world in.

Abuja 2017

Eka Sunny Akpaidiok

Your heart is mine

Many years gone by
Much time also
My soul yearns for you
My body craves for yours
My mind seeks to blend
With all you are

Come home quick
For my heart still ticks
Home is where the heart is
Your heart is mine.

April 2016.

The Tide of Time

When the day is gone, and the night draws near
When my back is bent, and the cane gone crooked
Perhaps it won't hurt to know who's out there
Waiting for me; to lend a helping hand

Springtime and summer
The lilies sprout
The petals wither

Autumn and winter
Leafy ground, crackle, *crackles*
Ice cold, frosty air.

The day fades into shades of grey
The night birds soon will all asleep
The music of time faints away an echo
Soon my song will end and the lids shut.

Calabar, 1993

Eka Sunny Akpaidiok

Friendship

Time
Courage
Guts

An open mind
A huge heart
Willingness
To love
Be hurt

Risk yourself
Lose yourself
Give all
Be all.

Abuja, 2017

Hush!

July

Slowly it creeps on you.
Stealthily…
Deceptively…
No warning
It's here

You ask yourself
Where did all that time go?

It's the seventh
Perfection
Possibilities
No limits
July!

Welcome.

Abuja, July 2017

Eka Sunny Akpaidiok

Secrets

How do you tell them?
A secret kept for years
Yet you long to unburdened
And be free to smile again

Will they understand? Empathize?
Would their minds comprehend? Why?
Nobody sought your opinion then
A cross to bear that was not yours

To grin and bear and a hide a pain
To smile and cheer like nothing amiss
You're trapped in a box, without air
You choke on your spittle, your mouth sour

I seek freedom. I yearn for redemption.
I seek light for the deadness of my soul
"Let me go" a voice within cries
Too long is long, my time is now.

Abuja 2016

The Art of

If you can only stay with me
If you would pause and see
If you would just hear me so speak
Not guilty as you make it out to be

If you can hold your breath
If you would be still a moment or two
If you would wait and not haste away
Not callous as you make it out to be

If you can give me a chance
If you would listen to the unspoken
If you would catch a twinkle in my eyes
Not serious as you make it out to be

If you can come away with me
If would hold on to the trust I give
If you would walk with me a mile more
Not scary as you make it out to be.

Abuja, May 2019.

Eka Sunny Akpaidiok

Love

Love now, not later
Love hard, show you care
Hide it not
Don't play tough
Be vulnerable
Weak if you can
Be gentle and kind hearted
Think not of yourself.

Love now, not later
Love patiently love waiting
Be slow
Take the time to show
Lose yourself
Ask the other.

Abuja 2015

Hush!

Love Alliances

He winked
She blinked
He beckoned
She moved
He stared
She blushed.

Eyelids dropped
Heartbeat stopped
At what could possibly be?
For all the world to see
A romance unfathomed
An unlikely alliance
Paired with some defiance
Between the north and the south.

Eka Sunny Akpaidiok

Hope Alive

I know you want to see me hitched
With all the trimmings summed
That tall glass of drinking water
Perhaps you will, I cannot say yet

I know you want to wear the colours
And dance to the rhythm of the beat
To hoot and howl and clap when asked
If you are patient you just might see

I know you can't wait to hear the news
Of my ungainly gait and morning upsets
Your bags are packed; you're a call away
Wait I say, soon enough you will come.

Abuja, October 2017.

Knowing

When you can see me sway in your eyes
And hear your name; a whisper on my breath

Till I can define your musky smell
And tell you apart from a mile away

When my words reveal your thoughts
And your tongue completes the words

Till every wrinkle tells a clear story
And every line is very well earned

When every mask of fear is unveiled
And every lie is put to shame

Till nothing shakes the bond we have
And love covers every error or sin

Then you know.

Abuja, February 2017

Eka Sunny Akpaidiok

The Promise

Blow a kiss
Whisper nothings
Make me sway

Let my head be heady
From your promises full
Touch my palms
Give me your trust

Stare into my eyes
Glean the truth in them
Excuse the lips fraught
Listen to my heartbeat

Butterflies flit and fly
My tummy makes music
I will feel better
If you will let me be

The promise of a kiss
My deep longing
The hope of our dream
Let the lids together be.

Abuja, 2018

Seeking

Sometimes across a bright rainbow
There is a promise of a day tomorrow
Somewhere on the side of the nation
There is a love as deep as the ocean

Speak out of things phantom
You break my heart when you do
For then I long for the impossible
Try hard as you may, you are unrequited

Why stir a love not ready?
Why share with me the longings?

February 2019

Eka Sunny Akpaidiok

My Hearts Cry Desire

I yearn

The essence of quietness
To be still in Your presence
Your gentle whisper to hear

The need of prayer
To bow my knees before You
Your face to seek while I can

To know You is my one desire
To see You is what I crave
To worship You is all I live for
To hear You I pray

Let me be
Let me see

The child You want me to be

Let me stand tall
In all still stand

Calabar, August 2000
Another place in seasons of innocence

Closer

Take my hand
I am here
Hold me close
Don't ever let go
Trust me now
Cause I'm forever
Look to me
Don't drop your gaze

For I'm your God
And you are mine
I'm your King
All the time
So take my hand
Don't ever let go
Hold me close
I'm here for you.

Abuja, April 2019

Eka Sunny Akpaidiok

He Speaks

In whispered tones and distinct notes
Still in thunderous clouds
And Crackling leaves

In lyrical music and unabashed laughter
On word filled pages
And hungry faces

In rushing whirlwind, on a hail rainy day
On the mountain peak
And cascading waterfalls

Do you not hear?
Perceive not
The sound
Unmistakably?

In dense forests and animal parks
In whistling pines
And a roaring sea

In quick footsteps and brisk walks
In chirping birds
And croaking frogs

In beating hearts and still breaths
In unasked questions
And confused minds

In hollow dark caves reechoing
On rocky hills uneven
And pesky bees

In quiet days and boring silence
In monotones
And somber voices
In dry retorts and rib cracking jests
In wise dialogues

Hush!

And common sense.

He speaks…still.

Eka Sunny Akpaidiok

Rapture

The trumpet sounds
The archangels' call
Dead in Christ rise
Alive in Him
Caught up!

We would see Him
Face to face
Behold His glory
Be with Him
Touch!

What moment
Glorious
Exciting
Rapture!

The streets of gold
The pearly gates
A heavenly mansion
Fresh clean air

Hmm!

A deep breath…

Calabar, 1998

Dusk

Eka Sunny Akpaidiok

Mscheew!

I refuse to be shocked
Any more
By all that's happening
And would continue to happen

I refuse to be moved
And worry myself to nuts
Over the misbehaviours
Of those who should know better

I refuse to care and fret now and then
Over the shenanigans
Of those I once held in high esteem

To the boot I say
I don't care a hoot
Be caught in the act
See if I care

If today I hear
You have gone deep end
Not an eye would I blink
A thick skin
I've got on now

So I say to all the

Dopers
Panama paperians
FIFA scandalous
Non-asset declarers
Public office looters
Pipeline vandals
Boko Haramists
Cheating Athletes
Lying Ministers

Hush!

Unashamed Presidents, etc, etc

I am not shocked
My mouth is closed
My lips a thin line
My gaze unflinching
I am resolute in my stance
Cause I've had it up to here
Be caught in the act
I reiterate
See if I care
Mscheew!

April 2016
One gum dropping shocking happening.
One too many

Eka Sunny Akpaidiok

Career Talk

Hospitality industry
Fixed smile on lips
Dropped attitude
Raised eyebrows
Be nice even forced
Learned to give way
The customer is right

Political politicians
Learnt to double speak
With tongue in cheek
Diplomacy at a high price
Bare faced lies that
Weighed heavily on conscience
Still with the skill to go on
Like nothing ever happened

Those NGOs
Money and intentions
Monitoring, interventions
Evaluations, Projections
All getting in the way
Insisting to be heard
"It's about the people", they cried out

Public service abused
Amazed at the bureaucracy
Red tape, slow pace and ugly
The beehive of gossip
The haters club, the vengeful ones
Be careful whom you cross
Keep your chair safe
Carry the olive with you
Douse your space a lavish amount

Sold a thing or two
Carried merchandise and touted
With no nerve to pursue the debts

Hush!

Was bold to tell myself the truth
A desk, laptop and office space
I'm all about. Get me one
And I'll make yours come true

Abuja 2016

Eka Sunny Akpaidiok

Judged

What we eat
What we wear
What we don't eat
What we don't wear
Where we live
Where we go
Who we're seen with

If we are married
Why we are not married
Who we married
Whether we have children
Why we don't have children
Why we can't have children

If we have money
How we made our money
What we do with our money
How we spend our money

How big our house is
What we have in them
What area we live in

If we vacation
Where we vacation
What friends we have
Which ones we keep
What car we drive
How many we own

What schools we went
Which ones our kids attend
If we throw a party
Who we invited

Hush!

Which restaurant we eat in
Which hotels we stay in
Where we work
How much we earn...exhausting!
Judged!

Eka Sunny Akpaidiok

Escape

Their warm embrace washes over my dark soul
The beauty of innocence not lost, not spoilt
A soft sigh escapes my cracked lips
My pain is soothed, and soon I'm at ease

I linger in their presence and hope for no end
I join in their laughter and unending questions
Why, how, when, what, which, this, that.
Life is easy without the cluttered clutter of my mind

Cascades of waves beat across my heart
Let me go far away…

January 2017

Signs and Time

When do you know you've had enough?
Of this life that rules your soul
Body strong, Grip firm
Quick on the feet
Grace like the gazelle

Three dozens and a bit
You'd think by now
You should know
Your name is control

Perhaps it's time
To rest the racket
And not break it

Wait..
Pick up the broken
Tomorrow comes again
This life that rules your soul

Abuja 2018

Eka Sunny Akpaidiok

At last!

It looked like it would never come
We hurried and buried ourselves
All the while longing for home
We dragged our weary selves

Our true story lies in the journey we made
Our testimonies seen in the prayers said
And while we went as we were bade
We leaned on the One who for all paid

Today we gather not of ourselves
With upraised hands and lifted faces
We refuse to remain as dust on shelves
We have come to take our rightful places

What a privilege! What honour!
Receive glory tonight LORD
Dwell in the midst of your people
Inhabit our praise, Delight in our worship

Abuja 2018

Past

Yesterday my sun came out
Its light shone on my dark past
Its back warmed from its heat

Pain as deep as an ocean
Hurt that leaves you breathless

I will sing my song and do my dance
I will laugh hard and not dwell on the past
Not easy I know yet still doable you see
For pain will linger if you let it

Yesterday my sun came out
And memories of old assailed
It wrapped its heat around me
And my burned within my mind.

Abuja 2017

Eka Sunny Akpaidiok

Ambushed

Crack, whip
Bang clang
Blow thud
Jab, grab

Rough voices
Coarse notes
Painful grip
Fierce gaze

Quick out
Snatch bag
Smash phone
Zoom off!

June 2017

Hush!

Stay Alive

The other day the doctor came
And touted a big name

He scared the living light off me
"Hypoxia" he said you see!

So off I went to check it up
Alas I tripped over the cup

Water spilled all around the place
And I got some on my face.

"This is not what I need" I cringed
Not even when I binged!

But perhaps it will help the dehydration
And set me on a mission.

This crisis that I inherit so
Sorely needs a place to go
"Oxygen" I thought out loud
Oh Lord let my thoughts not becloud

Though cold fear grips my heart
I always knew right from start,

That hope and blood I will need to fight
This curse with all of my might

Abuja, March 2019

Eka Sunny Akpaidiok

People

Just that, people
Frail, humans who fall and fail
Not perfect; they shock and amaze
Let down and leave you breathless
Amuse and surprise, astound and disappoint.

People:
Just that, people
Don't hold too much in high esteem
When they stumble, you hurt yourself
Leave room for doubts, believe God more

People;
Just that, people
Mere mortals who perish any day soon
One minute we laugh, the next we cry
Today we bless, tomorrow we curse

People:
Just that, people
Not afraid to live, love and be loved
Humour, laughter, joyous, fun loving
Free spirited, spiritual beings.

December 2018

Hush!

Caution!

Lots of opinions in the air
Agendas with not much to spare
Would we but stop and think
We just might be on the brink

A war of words, the pen as they say
Mightier than the sword, let it pay
Cross the *t,* dot the *i,* lace with grace
Build the peace with each pace

Two sides to every coin there was
Neither right nor wrong if we pause
A differing of opinions each entitled
These old men are but recycled.

February 2019

Eka Sunny Akpaidiok

Stolen

A certain time a daring thief came
Not at night as we all had thought
Whether in the day it's all the same
He took the glue for which we fought

This thief hid not his ugly face
Neither did he see the red shame
He stole away like one with grace
Was bold to even leave a name

He stole the glue that bound
Trampled on our dignity and pride
He took our voices and sound
Leaving us like an unrequited bride

Our nature he has studied so well
Our times he has on his fingertips
Our moods he pretty can truly tell
In a word he breathes from his lips

We lose sight of what is true
We bicker of over what is not
We snarl till our faces turn blue
Denying we're all we have got.

Abuja 2019.

Hush!

Only then

When the night is quiet
And the silence deafens
When my phone is still
And friends let me be

I will watch.

Abuja 2019.

Eka Sunny Akpaidiok

Forward

I can beat myself black or blue
It does not change or make anything new
I can wrings my hands and almost draw blood
It makes no difference if it becomes a flood
Forward is what I should do next
I had this written long ago in text

His mission was my passion
His creation my vision

I am caught in the moment when words fail
And I beat my arms and wring my hands in
Forward is what I should do next
I had this written long ago in text

Abuja 2019.

Hush!

Notes

Slowly the notes recede...
m:m: r:d:d:t:s:l:s:f:m
m: f: f: f: f: f: f: f: m: s: d
A faint echo now I hear
Away in a manager
Let the Magnificat goest.
m:s:s:s:f:m:f:r:r:m
d: d: t: d:
Sleep cometh at last!

December 2016

Eka Sunny Akpaidiok

Saying Goodbye

I waited for you to come
Longingly I held out my hands
I sniffed at the air as the wind changed
I drank in that earthy smell from your first drops

"Did you do as I requested?"
"Did you spare us when you fell?"
Would I but speak for myself?
Others may not testify

Now with mixed feelings I watch as you go
Nostalgic, reminiscent of the times I watched
As you raged, and raved and threatened to
And I am reminded of how I yearned

The months have rolled by
The weeks are far spent
The dust are gathering
Too quickly if you ask

But what can I say? We are all the same
Longing for the next, forgetting the old
Forgive my treacherous heart
Alas the new is new

Fret not, don't lose no sleep
All too soon we all will forget
When the tide changes
I will yearn for you...again

Abuja, November 2016

Becoming

When we are old and losing our marbles
And our carriers no longer hold weight
When I look across the time and space
And see your wrinkled face
Would I see you I once knew
Or cringe in fear at the fading new?

When my breath reeks of old
And my hands twitch from pain
When my ears hear only what I say
When I look across time and space
And the curtains raise the light
Would my jaw still drop at the beaming sight?

When sometimes I snap out in fear
For we are becoming what we know not
When my mind is befuddled with yesterdays
Of memories I can't remember
When I look across time and space
Will your words still leave a trace?

When I lie down still in breath
And my skin in a hue all too well
When my heartbeat no longer in tune
And the light shines ever so bright
When I look across time and space
Will I see you would I embrace?

Abuja 2019

Eka Sunny Akpaidiok

November

It's the eleventh.
Time to judge
Stop and count
the manyBlessings
Time tobe grateful
to cast your mind
see how farHe's brought you
Time to sayThank you
Remember a kind deed
Write a letter, Sing a song
Break out in dance
Rejoice. Laugh.
Call a few friends
Visit the family
Lay the table
Carve the turkey
Stop the hustle
Hush the bustle
Drum rolls please

November... Thanksgiving

Welcome!

November

Hush!

Not Done

Victory at last.
Mission accomplished.
Bone tired.
Feet dragging
Summoned
Half asleep
Every muscle screaming for help
Tempted to say
'I'm done for the year'
Looking for that spot
Can't sing to save my life
But...
There is still some time
Left
Still levels to change
School runs to make
Diapers to change
Heights to climb
Hectic schedules
Crazy drives
One last prayer
Before the year
Turns over
And sprouts
A new leaf.

December 2016

Eka Sunny Akpaidiok

The Breaking of

To seasons like no other
To moments without bother
To ease and grace
Even in feminine pace
To heights attainable
And blazing trails
To a new you

Welcome!

Hush!

Dawn

Eka Sunny Akpaidiok

New Day

It is okay to weep
Does not mean you're weak
It is okay to vent out
Just says you peaked

But when you're done weeping
'Cause the tears will dry up
and when your voice grows coarse
from all the rage and rant

It's time to rise
Wipe away the tears
Clear out your throat
Take a step forward
Into the bright new day.

Abuja 2016

Hush!

Go figure!

They don't want you up,
Don't stay down

They don't want you smiling
Stretch your lips a mile wide

They want you in shame
Don't give them the chance

They want you in the dark
Shine your light brighter

They don't want you trying
Don't give up on you

They don't want you succeeding
Give the victory sign

They want you in the dumps
Don't give them the pleasure

They want you failing
Live to try again!

December 2018

Eka Sunny Akpaidiok

No Fool

I might look cute and all
I might act like I got it all
Don't be fooled
Just be cool
Show me love
Now and forever.

Abuja 2016

Thanksgiving

To God be the glory for years gone by
Most times together, sometimes apart
Our thoughts, our dreams, moments and triumphs
To God be the glory

These years come and gone
We might as well been dreaming
Where did it all go?
We would be asking

To God be the glory for years gone by
Some sad some happy
Exciting moments and dull ones
To God be the glory for years gone by
An everyday affair, something new to share

Quiet days, noisy hours
Smiles and frowns
We shared them all

Our fights, our joys
Our cries and laughter
On cold nights and warm days
To God is the glory for years gone by.

Calabar, 1998

Eka Sunny Akpaidiok

Life

I hear the sound of laughter
Unbridled, not restrained
It has a lilting sound
Like music to the ear

Children frolicking in the sand
Playing hide and seek
The innocence of babes
Untouched, not spoilt

I watch as two stroll pass
Whispering what I know not
There is queerness about them
Green with envy, I almost hiss

My nostrils itch, as I perceive
A scent so mouth watering
I gravitate towards it like a fly
It's mama putting the meal of the day

I let my hands feel the tendrils
Soft, curly; the creator's gift
A new gift, shiny, untainted
By the world's stress

I revel at the taste of the bite
Deep succulent and juicy
Dripping off the first rains
I sink in my teeth.

Abuja 2016

Girl

I am she, I am her
I am formed like an eight
I take, I give
I bear the weight
Through wear and tear

My life is not easy
The other won't let it
But I insist, for I am strong
I will not stay down.

Do you think me weak?
Fragile and hopeless
You see me as nothing
You trample on my dignity

Watch it, I say to you
You know not whom you dare.

October 2017

Eka Sunny Akpaidiok

The Morning Comes

I stayed up all night
Doing what I thought right
Why I bother I'll never know
Cause at the end I reap what I sow

All night I waited for the morning light
Strained my eyes with all of my might
This is not my thing I must confess
Sooner or later it will all become a mess

Hope arose as the sun came into sight
It shone so clear, an all new bright
Gladly I welcomed it my way
Perhaps still I will have my say.

December 2018

Coming Out Strong

Don't be fooled by my docile stance
My pert smile that hides the quivering of my lips
Think not that I am comfortable
With all your bad behavior
A doormat you have trampled on me
These years I served, despising myself
Soon enough I will rise like the phoenix
Take my life in at the slightest chance.

Abuja 2017

Eka Sunny Akpaidiok

No Doubts

This battle will be fought
Whether liked or not

Even in this trite confusion
There will be a transfusion

Though the cells be red or blue
And the pain leaves not one clue

My body writhes in sore pain
And I wonder if I'm still sane

Let me go, from this side so full of care
To a far place where I can let down my hair

I am weary from your needle
From *hypoxia*, *thalassema* and being feeble

NO! I am resilient and strong
I refuse to go without a song.

Abuja, March 2019

Light the Earth

Light the earth with a smile
Don't let the hurt steal your light
Give of yourself the calm within
Soothe away the ugly pain
Be still your beating heart
Let the lines not crease.

Abuja 2016

Eka Sunny Akpaidiok

Safe

Yet you love me
Always mindful of me
Never cease to amaze me
That is why I exclaim.

My name in your palms
Secured on all sides
Your name my retreat
Unafraid is my place

Abuja 2017

Hush!

Civic Duty

Men in flowing gowns cry out their intentions Promises of heaven here on this side of earth.
We believe; howbeit naively to the polls we go Civic duty it's called, so I am told
The crowds gathered, did we have a choice?
The grind was ugly, the situation grime
"Line up" they said, "take numbers" they ordered. After a while, neither worked!
Blazing sun and parched throats, braved out like zombies to the lot
Hawked drinks and free side dishes Middle - aged broads brought along
If you sniffed your way at them
They served a plate and a dash of smile
Hired hands in brown slacks and gummy boots
Did not look so bright as they worked
Lash extensions melted away by the heat
One still had one on and blinked ever so rapidly
"Off with the darn thing," the people touted *"Perhaps you might get some real work done!"*
A damsel in distress sashayed her way to the line
She bared her teeth and winked at the men He shifted and dared to create some space Her behind looked good enough for a ride
Claws drawn out like daggers at a duel Females hissed out in tune like crazed fire
"Don't you dare" the message passed
 Now tempers had flared like those gassed
The hustle is real even on the civic line!

Abuja 2019
To be continued...

Eka Sunny Akpaidiok

Arise Nigerians

Do we keep quiet because we are afraid?
If we uttered and said what we knew
They come for us with clubs and knives
Sometimes not so obvious for the eye to see

Come let us go to the square and shout
Let our voices be heard and our hearts felt
Injustice everywhere, hunger in the land
Who will speak up for my father's children?

They came promising in their flowing '*agbadas*'
Earnestly they vowed to take us to the Promised Land
They spoke of power, of roads, and water, and food
They sweated, they cajoled, their voices grew coarse

Vain words, indecent proposals, shiny looking notes
Like one drugged, zombies, a spell was cast on us
We drank in their words, greedy for what we heard
No clue, no vision; we did not see beyond our noses

Weeks have rolled by, months long gone now
Soon we are counting years, wondering when
Another round has come, time to throw the dice
Would we get it right this time, to ask the question?

Speak up; do not be fooled again, man
Stand up; insist on what is right and fair
Brace up, now not later, now is to do
Your vote, your say. Your vote, your power.

Abuja 2017

Changed Narratives

Change the sordid narrative
Without a lot of palliatives
Tell the truth in all the places
Corruption does wear many faces

In stolen mandates aided by rigged votes
In greased palms along unsafe highways
In dirty classrooms and unmarked notes
In cramped clinics and unwashed trays

In broken homes with failed dreams
In market stalls with expired creams
In church sermons spewing fake miracles
In hunted covens and deadbeat oracles

In corridors of power with uncertainty lurking
In government officials and their thieving aides
In show business and lecherous men skulking
In brides and grooms and their unlucky maids

Change the narrative; it's not too late
For this old tune has gone on long enough
With a party such as this, alive and to date
Switch up the music and have a good laugh

Corruption here and there, so they say
Is that really all that ails us so?
A great divide threatens our way
A sage said once, you reap what you sow

In our fading culture and all we hold dear
In our words where we are fast losing sleep
In our children's innocence hanging in fear
In our lack of mutual respect gone way deep

We tear at one another and forget our manners
We cast slurs and refuse to remember we know better
We have sunk so low, despicable us

Eka Sunny Akpaidiok

We dare accuse, when we are no better
We have all become corrupt
With our different faces
In our varied places.

Abuja 2019.

Hush!

I carry the green

Perhaps there were missed opportunities
Maybe regret or two
I know not if ever a red or blue
Or any other hue
Will grace my purse

But I sit today and think deeply
And realize with a jolt!
I am proud. I'm excited. I'm thrilled
I carry the green

So you sit there hissing and smirking,
Rolling your eyeballs and raising its brow
More pity for you as I shake my head
Go look for your own pride
This is mine.

October 2017

Eka Sunny Akpaidiok

Spirit and Truth

They call me frail and from dust
With no sail and somewhat lost
My path not defined as they say
For still I cannot find my way

Dripped in sin, shame rips me apart
Yet He loved me right from the start
He stopped by and gazed deeply
And my soul held truth barely

But I am;
Made like no other, no afterthought here
Molded to specifications, a wonder
Masterpiece from the beginning
Set after the Father's heart

So set me free with your truth
Give me life with your spirit
For I hear a voice, still and small
Calling, Seeking; Saying

You are;
Created for this purpose
Made for this reason
Built for this moment

"Worship me in Spirit and Truth."

August 2018

Hush!

Tomorrow

The next day and the days to come...

Let the winners be humble
And the losers not stumble
Let the victor's chant not drown
And the waspish not frown

You know this is just the beginning
Much work lies with the winning...

On no particular day
For all years to come.

Eka Sunny Akpaidiok

The Blessing

Let our light not grow dim
Let our joy be full and infectious

May the sun stand still
At our very command

And the moonlight beam
On every dark path

Let the heavens open
Let blessings rain

Hush!

Dance

Break forth in dance
Sing out in joy
Embrace your morning
Your victory is nigh

Smile your heart out
Leap believing

For the time is nigh
Your time is here

Rise from the deep
Cast off the sack
Open your ears; listen
The music plays

The dance beat of victory.

Abuja May 2018

Eka Sunny Akpaidiok

Created

Bless the LORD, Bless the LORD
For unto Him we gather
Unto Him not of ourselves
To give thanks
To smile
To rejoice and share our hearts

From beginning LORD you knew us
Before our mothers conceived us
Even before we could utter a word
You laid us out like the foundations of the earth

Intricately woven like a bright coloured tapestry
Laid out like fine silk, bone to bone, flesh and nerves
Created, fearfully and wonderfully made
Fashioned after your own image

Right here, Right now, with lifted hands
Up raised praise as we gaze into your face
We will break out into a dance and shout out a song
For beauty, for life, for health you give

Bless the LORD, Bless the LORD
For unto Him we gather
Unto Him not of ourselves
We welcome You, LORD, Take your place.

Amen

September 2017

Hush!

Saying Thank You...

To God Almighty for life and inspiration,

To my parents for enlightening, encouraging and introducing me to words,

To my siblings; *BB, Nke and Bombom...my sounding boards,*

To all my family members and teachers,

To Prof. Eka Braide for editing the initial manuscript,

To Senator George Thompson Sekibo for being an inspiring example,

To Pastor Sarah Omakwu who stopped midway in a sermon one fine Sunday morning and said, *'Eka make it happen.'*

Tomy friends who reminded me...,

...And to everyone who waited to see this come to pass, the lid is off, the banks burst!

www.ingramcontent.com/pod-product-compliance
Lightning Source LLC
Chambersburg PA
CBHW051427150726
48000CB00005B/1980